VENEZUELA AS AN EXPORTER OF
4TH GENERATION WARFARE INSTABILITY

The past several years have marked the beginning of a different security era than that to which we are accustomed. Accordingly, this era requires a new orientation. Whether we like it or not, whether we want it or not, and whether we are prepared for it or not, the United States and the West are engaged in a number of unconventional, undeclared, and undefined asymmetric wars. If left ignored and unchecked, these wars compel radical, unwanted, and epochal political-economic-social change. Even if that compulsion is generally indirect, ambiguous, conducted over long periods of time, and not perceived to be as lethal as land conventional maneuver war, that does not alter the cruel reality of the compulsion.[1]

Since his election as the President of Venezuela in 1998, Hugo Chavez has encouraged and continues to encourage his Venezuelan, Latin American, Russian, and Iranian partners to support an undeclared asymmetric war paradigm designed to put an end to U.S. political and economic influence in the Western Hemisphere and to transform the whole of Latin America into a single Bolivarian (Socialist) state. Chavez's model centers on a three-front asymmetric war that is: 1) psychological-political; 2) uses combinations of asymmetric ways and means to achieve its ends; and, 3) is deliberately protracted. In addition to Asymmetric War, Chavez calls this type of conflict 4th Generation War (4GW).[2]

Whether or not Chavez can deliver on his three-front 21st-century transition program is really not all that important. This is not because this is the rhetoric of a "nut case," a "clown," or even a "dead man" immersed in "political theater." This is, importantly, the rhetoric of an astute warrior who understands asymmetric war and who is performing the traditional and universal Leninist-Maoist function of providing a strategic vision and operational plan for a successful revolutionary conflict. Most importantly, Hugo Chavez's Bolivarian dream has stirred the imaginations of many Latin American and other interested observers around the world. He has provided a seductive Leninist blueprint for a utopian future. Anyone can take it, adapt it for his own use, and use it anywhere in the world to bring about radical political, economic, and social change. Thus, it appears that Chavez is prepared to help friends, partners, and allies to destabilize, to facilitate the processes of state failure, and to "destroy in order to build" in true revolutionary fashion.[3] Moreover, according to Chavez, it does not matter whether or not he will be able to continue to direct that effort. He states straightforwardly that ". . . independent of my personal destiny, this revolution . . . has gotten its start, and nothing and no one can stop it."[4]

To help strategic leaders—and anyone else who has the responsibility for dealing with, analyzing, planning, implementing, and/or reporting on contemporary security threats--understand this phenomenon, this monograph will address four cogent issues relevant to the context of President Chavez's grand strategic political-psychological destabilization effort. They are: 1) Hugo Chavez's Bolivarian Vision; 2) Key Components of the Chavez Strategic-Level Asymmetric Warfare Model; 3) The Paramilitary Operational Model for Compelling Radical Change in the Western Hemisphere; and, 4) Implications and Recommendations. Lastly, this would be a good point from which military and civilian leaders might start thinking about all the asymmetric wars that the United States and its allies face now and will continue to face in the future.

HUGO CHAVEZ'S BOLIVARIAN VISION AND HOW TO ACHIEVE IT

Almost no one seems to understand the Marxist-Leninist foundations of Hugo Chavez's political thought. It becomes evident, however, in his general vision of the Bolivarian Revolution. The abbreviated concept is to destroy the old foreign-dominated (U.S.-dominated) political and economic systems in the Americas, to take power, and to create a socialistic, nationalistic, and "popular" (direct) democracy in Venezuela that would sooner or later extend throughout the Americas.[5] Despite the fact that the possible use of military force is never completely separated from the Leninist concept of destroying bourgeois opposition, Chavez's revolutionary vision will not be achieved through a conventional military war of maneuver and attrition, or a traditional insurgency. According to Vladimir Lenin and Chavez, a "new society" will be created only by a gradual and systematic application of agitation and propaganda. That long-term effort is aimed at exporting instability and generating public opinion in favor of the "revolution" and against the bourgeois system.[6] Thus, the contemporary asymmetric revolutionary warfare challenge is rooted in the concept that the North American "Empire" and its bourgeois political friends in Latin America are not doing what is right for the people and that the socialist Bolivarian philosophy and leadership will.

In these terms, regime legitimacy is key to the conflict, and it is public opinion that is the main target of

3

the revolutionary effort. Chavez's vision comes at a time when, despite general economic progress, there are deep flaws in the democratic political systems throughout the Western Hemisphere. The relative popular dissatisfaction stems from deep-rooted socio-economic inequalities, distrust and lack of confidence in the police, national legislatures, and political parties. There are also rising popular expectations along with a popular consciousness of nonexistent rights.[7] The apparent waning of U.S. power has opened the possibility of a new global geopolitical order. At the same time, the worldwide financial crisis and the rise of the BRIC nations (Brazil, Russia, India, and China) have shaken the conventional wisdom that capitalism and liberal democracy are superior to the alternatives.[8] Latin America now—as in the 1960s and 1970s—appears to be a revolutionary's dream.

Five Enabling Concepts.

Hugo Chavez's Bolivarian strategic-level dream depends on five enabling concepts. It begins with the premise that traditional post-World War II socialist and Marxist-Leninist political-economic models made mistakes, but the theory remains valid. The idea is that representative democracy and the U.S.-dominated capitalism of the new global era are total failures. Representative democracy and capitalism serve only elites—not the common people. These failures must now be replaced by "participatory democracy," "direct democracy," or what some detractors have called "radical" or "neo-populism." In these terms, Chavez is: 1) re-elaborating a Rousseauan concept of "direct" or "totalitarian" democracy; and, 2) promoting a socialist economic system as two parts of a five-part overarching political-economic model for Latin America.[9] The other three parts of the model include: 3) a new security scheme for Venezuala; 4) social programs to strengthen "direct democracy" and its internal power base; and, 5) maximum communications support to the regime. That overall system of power is intended to ensure internal peace and societal harmony in Venezuela that will—in time—provide the foundations for a Hemisphere-wide regional power bloc, and socioeconomic and political integration.[10]

Direct Democracy and the Socialist Economic System. The current concept of Venezuelan democracy has its roots firmly in the French Revolution and subsequent perversions of the Rousseauan notion of "total" (totalitarian) democracy. In this scenario, the individual surrenders his rights and personal interests to the state in return for the enforcement of social harmony and the General Will. Prior to the French Revolution, kings ruled by "Divine Right" and were sovereign. With the revolution, however, sovereignty was shifted from the king to the nation-state. Thus, the state enjoys absolute power (*de facto* sovereignty)—through the enforcement of Rousseau's General Will—as an essential right.[11]

The main tenets of direct democracy in contemporary Venezuela dictate that: 1) the new authority in the state must be a maximum leader who communicates directly with the people, interprets their needs, and emphasizes "social expenditure" to guarantee the legitimate needs and desires of the people; 2) elections, Congress, and the courts will provide formal democracy and international legitimacy (*de jure* sovereignty), but will have no real role in governance or the economy; 3) the state will control or own the major means of national economic production and distribution; and,

4) the national and regional political-economic integration function will be performed by the supreme leader by means of his regional financial, material, informational, and political-military support of radical populist and 21st-century social movements.[12]

The Security Scheme. Lacking the conventional power to challenge the United States or most of Venezuela's immediate neighbors, President Chavez and his followers know that asymmetric conflict is a logical means of expression and self-assertion. It is a concept as old as war itself, a methodology of the weak against the strong. The primary characteristic of asymmetric conflict is the use of disparity between contending parties to gain advantage. Strategic asymmetry has been defined as "acting, organizing, and thinking differently than opponents in order to maximize one's own advantages, exploit an opponent's weaknesses, attain the initiative, or gain greater freedom of action and movement. It can have both psychological as well as physical dimensions."[13] Chavez's concept of asymmetric war makes explicit the need to generate a mix of unconventional methods that authoritatively integrates a nation-state's political, economic, social-moral, informational, and military instruments of power. This type of conflict is not won by seizing specific territory militarily or destroying specific industrial or nuclear capabilities. It is won by altering the political-psychological-economic-social factors that are most relevant in a targeted culture. But, like all others, this kind of conflict is intended to resist, oppose, gain control of, or overthrow an existing government or symbol of power—and bring about radical political change. All this requires a complete unity of effort by the state, using the multidimensional instruments of national and international (alliances and partnerships) power that it has at its disposal.[14]

Thus, the Venezuelan Constitution of 1999 provides political and institutional autonomy for the armed forces, under the absolute control of the President and commander in chief. President Chavez has also created an independent national police force, outside the traditional control of the armed forces, which is directly responsible to the President. At the same time, efforts have gone forward to establish a one million-person military reserve and two additional paramilitary organizations — the *Frente Bolivariano de Liberacion* (Bolivarian Liberation Front) and the *Ejercito del Pueblo en Armas* (Army of the People in Arms). The armed forces and the police perform traditional national defense and internal security missions within the context of preparing for what President Chavez has called a "4th Generation Asymmetric War of All the People."[15] The military reserve and the paramilitary (militia) organizations are charged to: 1) protect the country from a U.S. or Colombian invasion with an Iraqi-style insurgency; 2) act internally as armed, anti-opposition militias; and, 3) act internationally as armed anti-bourgeois militias.[16] The institutional separation of the various security organizations ensures that no one security institution can control the others, but the centralization of those institutions under the control of the President ensures his absolute control of security and "social harmony" in Venezuela — and elsewhere.[17]

Social Programs and Communications. To strengthen his personal position and internal power base, President Chavez is spending large amounts of money on an amorphous Plan Bolivar 2000 for the building and renovation of schools, clinics, day nurseries, roads, and housing for the poor. Additionally, the President is developing education and literacy outreach programs, agrarian reform programs, and workers' cooperatives. At the same time, he has established MERCAL, a state company that provides subsidized foodstuffs to the poor. Chavez has also imported 16,000 Cuban doctors to help take care of the medical needs of the Venezuelan underclass. Clearly, these social programs offer tangible benefits to the mass of voting Venezuelans who were generally ignored or neglected by previous governments.[18]

The intent of the communications and informational efforts is to generate strong and favorable public opinion. Thus, *Bolivarianismo* requires maximum media (radio, TV, and newspapers/magazines) support to purvey ideas, develop mass consensus, and generate electoral successes. Ample evidence exists that Chavez-controlled media are using emotional arguments to gain attention, to exploit real and imagined fears of the population, to create outside enemies as scapegoats for internal failures, and to inculcate the notion that opposition to the regime equates to betrayal of the country. President Chavez's personal involvement in the communications effort is also clear and strong. Statements, speeches, and interviews are being broadcast throughout Venezuela, the Caribbean Basin, and large parts of Central and South America every day on the state-owned *Television del Sur*. Additionally, Iranian TV (Hispan TV) is now broadcasting in Spanish 24 hours a day throughout all of Latin America.[19]

Conclusions.

All these programs together provide the President of Venezuela—whoever he might be—with the architecture to generate a unity of effort among the various political-psychological-socioeconomic-infor-mational-military instruments of state power. That unifying structure, rather than traditional govern-mental hierarchy, allows the President a vastly more effective and efficient means through which to pursue his political-strategic Bolivarian objectives. At a mini-mum, Hugo Chavez has created the elements that can make Venezuela a regional power. He or his succes-sor can easily export direct democracy, oil money, socialist propaganda, and military assets to friendly governments, radical groups, and insurgents all over the Hemisphere. In these terms, Chavez is also devel-oping the capability to destabilize and force a radical restructuring of specific bourgeois political-economic systems over large parts of the Americas.[20] But, insta-bility is only a symptom, not the threat. Instability is the starting point from which to understand the sec-ond-, third-, and fourth-level effects that shape the Latin American security environment now and for the future. Instability also defines the ultimate security threat for now and the future—that is, the threat that no one likes to talk about—the export of economic and political instability to foment the state failure process.

KEY COMPONENTS OF THE CHAVEZ STRATEGIC-LEVEL ASYMMETRIC WARFARE MODEL

This type of conflict is primarily psychological-political and aimed at human terrain rather than geo-graphical territory. As a consequence, the new primary center of gravity (the hub of all power and movement) is not military. It is public opinion and leadership.[21] This kind of conflict is based on perceptions, beliefs, expectations, and dreams. The key components of

Chavez's strategic-level asymmetric warfare model can be understood within the context of a deliberate three-front grand strategic conflict that: 1) is primarily psychological-political; 2) uses combinations of military and nonmilitary, lethal and nonlethal, and direct and indirect ways and means to accomplish its ends; and, 3) is deliberately protracted (temporal).[22]

Psychological-Political War.

The term "propaganda" connotes the dissemination or promotion of ideas, doctrine, and practices to further one's cause or damage the opposition's cause. Most commonly, the term is used pejoratively to imply deception or distortion of the truth. Lenin and Chavez use the term in both senses. Because it is as important to protect one's own centers of gravity as it is to attack the enemy's, the intent is to indirectly and directly alter the political-psychological factors that are most relevant to one's own and targeted cultures. That is, to spread "a proper understanding of the present social and economic system . . . [and] an understanding of the historical task of international Social-Democracy" (21st-Century Socialism).[23] Inseparably connected with propaganda is agitation. Agitation means that small groups of individuals foment and take part in the various coercive manifestations of the revolution and "all the conflicts between workers and the capitalists."[24] Moreover, there is no issue in the political field that does not serve as a subject for political agitation." As a consequence, according to Lenin, small propaganda-agitator organizations ("agi-props") must be organized, trained, and utilized to support the political-psychological struggle and to act as the "midwives" of new social orders.[25] Together, propaganda and agitation will generate political-psychological-economic-social-military support for the whole revolutionary organization and for its immediate, intermediate, and ultimate objectives.[26]

The primary and specific effort, however, that ultimately breaks up and defeats an adversary's political-economic-social system and compels radical change is the multidimensional erosion of people's morale and political will.[27] The better one protagonist is at that persuasive-coercive (agi-prop) effort, the more effective that protagonist will be relative to the opposition.[28] Accordingly, as noted above, the center of gravity is an adversary's public opinion and political decisionmaking leadership.[29] The basic reality of this new center of gravity is that information and the media (propaganda), not military firepower or technology, is the primary currency upon which "modern war amongst the people" is run.[30] This political-psychological effort also defines victory or defeat. In these terms, public opinion and political leadership provide the architecture from which to develop a viable ends, ways, and means strategy that can win a prolonged multidimensional political-psychological war.

Combinations.

The two Chinese colonels who authored *Unrestricted Warfare*, Qiao Liang and Wang Xiangsui, are adamant. They unequivocally argue that regardless of whether a war took place 2,500 years ago or last year, the data indicate that all victories or failures display one common denominator—the winner is the national power, international alliance (power bloc), or nonstate political actor that is best organized and has implemented a combination of multidimensional efforts.[31]

The purpose of combinations is to organize a system of offensive and defensive power that is a great force multiplier and facilitator within the global security arena. This system gives new and greater meaning to the idea of a nation-state or other political actor using all available instruments of power to protect, maintain, and achieve perceived political and security interests.[32]

The dominating characteristic of a war of this kind is political-military, economic-commercial, or cultural-moral. Within the context of these combinations, there is a difference between the dominant sphere and the whole, although a dynamic relationship exists between a dominant type of general war and the supporting elements that make up the whole. As an example, Qiao and Wang state that conventional military war must be strongly supported by media (propaganda/information/moral) warfare and a combination of other types of war that might include but are not limited to psychological war, financial war, trade war, cyber war, diplomatic war, proxy war, narco-criminal war, and guerrilla war.[33] More specific examples of national power combinations include the following:

- Conventional military war/cyber war/media war (e.g., Georgia, 2008);
- Surrogate or proxy war/intelligence war/ media war (e.g., Lebanon, 2006);
- Narco-criminal war/financial war/psychological/media war (e.g., Mexico, to date);
- Guerrilla war/psychological-media war/narco-criminal war (e.g., Colombia and Peru, to date); and,
- Diplomatic war/media war/conventional war (e.g., Algeria, 1954-62).

Any one of the above combinations can be combined with others to form new methods and combinations of conflict. There are no means that cannot be combined with others. The only limitation is the imagination of the planner and decisionmaker. As a consequence, politically effective contemporary warfare requires the services of civilian warriors—as well as professional soldiers and policemen—who can conduct persuasion-coercion-propaganda war, insurgency war, media war, financial war, trade war, psychological war, network (virus) war, cyber war, chemical-biological-radiological war, etc. Professional soldiers no longer have a monopoly on power. Accordingly, civilian warriors must be included in the strategic architecture for contemporary warfare.[34]

Time as an Instrument of Statecraft.

Hugo Chavez and his disciples understand that war is no longer limited to using military violence to compel desired radical political-economic-social change. Rather, all means that can be brought to bear on a given situation must be used. A 4GW leader will tailor his actions to his adversaries' vulnerabilities, and to their psychological precepts.[35] In these terms, both Lenin and Mao taught that time (the long-term) becomes one of the main instruments of contemporary power. Prolonged war includes no place for compromise or other options short of achieving the ultimate political objective (radical political change). Lenin was straightforward: "Concessions are a new kind of war."[36] Thus, time is one more instrument of statecraft.

Moreover, because the "new" asymmetric conflict is generally political-psychological, protagonists must understand that it takes time to change peoples' minds and behavior and prepare them for phased, progressive moves toward short-and mid-term as well as long-term objectives. As examples, Mao and his Chinese communists fought for 28 years (1921-49); the Vietnamese communists fought for 30 years (1945-75); the Nicaraguan Sandinistas fought for 18 years (1961-79); and the Peruvian *Sendero Luminoso* organization has claimed that it is prepared to fight 75 years (1962-?) to achieve its revolutionary objective.[37] As a consequence, in 2005, Chavez claimed that he was planning for a protracted 40-year struggle in which he or other Bolivarian leadership must: 1) propagate Latin American nationalism; 2) educate, organize, and prepare several thousand professionals for organizational duties, combat, and governance who are prepared to lead the masses through a revolution and into the proverbial halls of power; and, 3) create a popular front not just of a few hundred "true believers," but a large number of Christians, Socialists, trade unionists, intellectuals, students, peasants, the "debourgeoised" middle classes, and friendly nations that will "march together to defeat sepoyan (lackey-like) militarism and U.S. imperialism."[38] Contrary to the teachings of some impatient revolutionaries who still adhere to the teachings of Che Guevara, no shortcut will work.[39]

Conclusions.

Hugo Chavez and his selected leadership understand that contemporary asymmetric war is not a kind of appendage (a lesser or limited thing) to the more comfortable conventional military attrition and maneuver warfare paradigms. It is a great deal more. Again, such war may be military or nonmilitary, lethal or nonlethal, or a mix of everything within a state or a coalition of states' (alliance) array of instruments of power. As such, it may be a zero-sum game in which only one winner emerges; or, in the worst-case scenario, no winner. It is, thus, total. That is to say, the "battlefield" is extended to everyone, everything, and everywhere — over time.[40]

Some important things in contemporary war have changed, but some have stayed the same. In 2005, we summarized the concept of modern asymmetric warfare by taking a page from a Harry Potter adventure. We called it "Wizard's Chess." As a metaphorical example, we further characterized Hugo Chavez as a "Master" of this deadly game. The analogy is still instructive and sobering:

> In that game, protagonists move pieces silently and subtly all over the game board. Under the players' studied direction, each piece represents a different type of direct and indirect power and might simultaneously conduct its lethal and non-lethal attacks from differing directions. Each piece shows no mercy against its foe and is prepared to sacrifice itself in order to allow another piece the opportunity to destroy or control an opponent — or to checkmate the king. Over the long-term, however, this game is not a test of expertise in creating instability, conducting violence, or achieving some sort of moral satisfaction. Ultimately, it is an exercise in survival. A player's failure in Wizard's Chess is death, and is not an option.[41]

The reality of this kind of "game" is grand strategic and epochal in scale, and ultimately witnesses the transition from one dominant political form to another. Politicized militias, hegemonic nonstate entities, and surrogates for traditional nation-states will likely move from war with some rules and conventions to new warmaking entities and into completely unrestricted warfare. Failing and failed states will possibly evolve into new and undesirable state forms such as rogue states, criminal states, draconian states (military dictatorships), neo-populist states (civilian dictatorships), or new "People's Republics." Failing or failed states may also dissolve and become parts of other states, or may be configured into entirely new entities.[42] In short, revolution is not an event; it is a process.

This takes us back to where we began. Hugo Chavez understands the sophistication and complexity of combinations of national instruments of power and alliances, and war as a whole. He also understands the value of facilitating the processes of state failure to achieve his objectives of establishing 21st-Century Socialism and Latin American *grandeza* (greatness). Chavez and his supporters understand the importance of dreams about survival and a better life for much of any given population. These are the bases of power—all else is illusion.

THE PARAMILITARY OPERATIONAL MODEL

Paramilitary operations to enable the three-front asymmetric war focus on: 1) six phases of varying levels of agi-prop activities; 2) the destabilization of the bourgeois enemy until his resolve is gone and the targeted country has reached failing or failed-state status; and, 3) generating a force multiplier by building alliances, partnerships, and coalitions. Abraham Guillen, one of Chavez's intellectual mentors, argued that these "political-[psychological]-moral factors are more decisive for victory than heavy armament and ironclad units."[43]

Six Phases that Elaborate "New" Roles of the Bolivarian Popular Militias.

General Gustavo Reyes Rangel Briceno articulated the six operational military/paramilitary phases of the program for the "liberation" of Latin America at his Change of Office Speech as Minister of Defense for the National Reserve and National Mobilization to take the higher post of Minister of [National] Defense. This speech, made on July 18, 2007, provided a 4GW asymmetric model to assist thinking about, planning, and implementing the Bolivarian dream. Accordingly, the general's speech might well have been written by Lenin, Abraham Guillen, or a younger Leninist mentor, Jorge Verstrynge.[44] Another aspect of the speech was quite clear. It was NOT written by a military officer steeped in the tradition of 3rd Generation Maneuver and Attrition War. It was NOT written by someone who was preparing his students or staff for an impossible war on the European or North American plains against hypothetical red-colored enemies who look, strangely, like Russian Combined Arms Armies. It was NOT written by someone whose purpose was to prepare his students or staff to fight the wars in Iraq and Afghanistan. General Briceno's speech, with its "new" phases, reflected "new" battlefields, "new" enemies, "new" forms of attack and defense, and "new" threats that are relevant to modern asymmetric wars of national resistance (strategic defense). Lastly, General Briceno's Change of Office Speech was written by an officer who was NOT looking for anything tangible. He was seeking the realization of a dream—the liberation of Latin America from the U.S. political-economic hegemon—a Marxian reward of history.[45]

Phase One: Destabilization of targeted societies through the exploitation of a combination of four types of war working within the context of the general war of resistance: 1) temporal (prolonged) war; 2) creating chaos and instability (governance war); 3) economic (finance and trade) war; and, 4) media (information/propaganda) war.

Phase Two: Create a popular (political) front out of the debourgeoised middle classes and other like-minded individuals to compete with and weaken a targeted government. The intent is to politically and psychologically support the four wars noted in Phase One.

Phase Three: Foment regional conflicts. This would involve covert, gradual, and preparatory political-psychological-military activities ("seeding operations") in developing and nurturing popular support for the war of resistance. The fomentation of regional conflicts over time would also involve the establishment and defense of "liberated zones" (quasi-states) within the state.

Phase Four: Plan and implement overt and direct intimidation activities, including popular actions (such as demonstrations, strikes, civic violence, personal violence, maiming, and murder) against feudal, capitalistic, militaristic opponents in particular and against *yanqui* imperialism in general. The intent is to debilitate targeted states and weaken bourgeois military command and control facilities.

Phase Five: Increase covert and overt political-psychological-economic-military actions directed at developing local popular militias to fight in their own zones, provincial or district militias to fight in their particular areas, and a larger military organization to fight in all parts of the targeted country with the cooperation of local and district militias.

Phase Six: Directly, but gradually, confront a demoralized enemy military force and bring about its desired collapse—or militarily invade a failing or failed state. The objective in either case would be to impose (compel) appropriate 21st-century socialist governance.[46]

Additionally, until the last moment in the third and decisive phase of the Latin American liberation process—when a targeted government is about to collapse—every action is preparatory work and not expected to provoke great concern from the enemy or its bourgeois allies. Only at the point of enemy collapse and the radical imposition of New Socialist governance will the people begin to enjoy the benefits of love, happiness, peace, and well-being.[47]

If this dream were to come true, Hugo Chavez or a successor would witness the metamorphosis of 15 or 20 Latin American republics into one great American nation. Experience demonstrates, however, that most political dreams very seldom come true (think of the 40+ years of Socialism in Eastern Europe, 1945-89). Ultimately, the international community must pay the direct and indirect social, economic, and political costs of state failure. As a consequence, the current threat environment in the Western Hemisphere is not a traditional security problem, but it is no less dangerous.[48]

Operationalizing a "New" Paramilitary Mission— Facilitating the Processes of State Failure.

Like revolution, state failure is a process, not an outcome. Contemporary 4GW asymmetric destabilization threats to personal and collective security and well-being are not necessarily direct attacks on a government. They are, however, proven means for weakening governing regimes. These indirect threats reflect a logical progression from the problems of institutional and state weaknesses to the partial collapse of the state, and, finally, to state failure. The process is brought on by poor, irresponsible, and/or insensitive governance and leads to one other fundamental reason states fail. That is, state failure can be a process exacerbated either by nonstate groups or nation-states (e.g., insurgents, transnational criminal organizations and their enforcer gangs, and/or civil or military or paramilitary organizations operating directly on behalf of a nation-state or indirectly as a proxy (surrogate). The general intent is to depose an established government or exercise illicit control over a targeted country. Destabilizing actions perpetrated by non-state groups (including proxies) or state authorities weaken government and its institutions, and regimes become progressively less capable of performing the fundamental security and well-being tasks of responsible governance.[49]

More specifically, the state failure process tends to move from personal violence to increased collective violence and social disorder to kidnappings, bank robberies, violent property takeovers, murders/assassinations, personal and institutional corruption, criminal anarchy, and internal and external population displacements. In turn, the momentum of this process of violence tends to evolve into more widespread social violence, serious degradation of the economy, and diminished governmental capability to provide personal and collective security and guarantee the rule of law to all citizens. Then, using complicity, intimidation, corruption, and indifference, an irregular political actor or nonstate group can quietly and subtly co-opt politicians, bureaucrats, and security personnel to gain political control of a given piece of the national territory. The individual or nonstate group that takes control of a series of networked pieces of such "ungoverned territory" can then become a dominant political actor (e.g., warlord) and control a quasi-state within a state.[50]

Somewhere near the end of the destabilization process, the state will be able to control less and less of its national territory and fewer and fewer of the people in it. The diminishment of responsible governance and citizen security generates greater poverty, violence, and instability—and a downward spiral in terms of socioeconomic development and well-being. It is a zero-sum game in which state, nonstate, or individual actors (e.g., insurgents, transnational criminal organizations, corrupt public officials, and hegemonic states) are the winners, and the rest of a targeted society are losers. Unless and until a society perceives that its government deals with issues of personal security, well-being, and socioeconomic development fairly and effectively, the potential for internal or external forces to destabilize and subvert a regime is considerable. Regimes that ignore this lesson often find themselves in a "crisis of governance." They face increasing social violence, criminal anarchy, terrorism, insurgency, and overthrow. This process has been known to lead to the violent imposition of a radical political-economic-social restructuring of the state and its governance in accordance with the values—good, bad, or non-existent—of the best organized and most-disciplined group left standing.

Another "New" Force Multiplier—Alliances, Partnerships, and Coalitions.

These are agreements among states or nonstate actors to: 1) coordinate behavior in the event of political-economic-social-military emergencies; 2) increase empirical power in the international security arena; 3) counterbalance threats posed by potential aggressors in the anarchical global security environment; and, 4) support coercive diplomacy. Thus, alliances, partnerships, and coalitions have operated in the security arena for thousands of years, and really are not "new" instruments of statecraft. Their primary rule and purpose, forever, has been and is to protect, maintain, and/or enhance one's own interests.[51]

These tenets define a part of Hugo Chavez's "New Strategic Map for the Exportation of the Bolivarian Revolution." That part of his "map" is entitled "Stimulating the New Multipolar System." The rationale for this is that "the United States will continue to increase its interventionist, aggressive, genocidal, and savage policies regarding the Americas. Thus, we must prepare ourselves to deal with and overcome these hegemonic issues. We must work hard, very hard, to prevail over the United States and extend the revolution to the rest of the Latin American region."[52] Accordingly, Chavez has brought together an unlikely assortment of state and nonstate actors, and criminal-terrorist organizations for these purposes. They are: 1) the Bolivarian Alliance led by Venezuala, which includes Bolivia, Cuba, Ecuador, Nicaragua, and, possibly, Argentina; 2) Iran and Russia; and, 3) at the very least, this alliance offers material and political support to the insurgent and drug trafficking Revolutionary Armed Forces of Colombia (FARC), Iranian surrogate and terrorist Hezbollah operations in the Western Hemisphere, and other violent nonstate actors such as African and Mexican Transnational Criminal Organizations (TCOs). Thus, this group of partners (allies) comprises a hybrid of state, nonstate, and criminal-terrorist franchises that appear to be expanding as this monograph is being written. The one thing this diverse group of parties has in common is a hatred for the West in general and the United States in particular.[53]

Alliance Enablers for the Exportation of Instability.

The operationalization of Chavez's "New Strategic Map for the Exportation of the Bolivarian Revolution" appears to be based on three mutually supporting alliance activities: 1) Combating International Isolation; 2) Increasing Economic Activism; and, 3) Increasing Paramilitary and Conventional Military Presence in the Hemisphere. Chavez and his disciples expect these 4GW alliance activities to lead to the destabilization of their bourgeois enemies. The "new" Socialist reasoning is quite realistic. "Adopting alliances is vital for the integration of Latin America because it is impossible for the United States [or anyone else] to use its vast conventional military force against them."[54]

Combating International Isolation. Alliances provide Venezuela with powerful friends both outside and inside the Western Hemisphere. The major allies have been noted above. Unofficial extra-hemispheric actors, in addition to Iran and Russia, would probably include China, Chinese Triads, African gangs and cartels, the Spanish Basque separatist organization (ETA), the Irish Republican Army (IRA), and various Islamic groups sponsored by Saudi Arabia and other Gulf

States to include al-Qaeda, Hamas, and Hezbollah.[55] A new element in the current configuration of forces in Latin America is that criminalizing states frequently use TCOs (cartels) as a form of statecraft. They bring these elements into areas of weak or no state sovereignty, and the TCOs and their enforcer gangs provide alternative (criminal) governance systems (quasi-states). Strategically, this alters the structure of global order and makes a lie of *de facto* or *de jure* sovereignty. This threat is operationalized by the illicit movement of goods (e.g., drugs, money, weapons systems, and human beings), and the billions of dollars that these illicit activities generate. The influence and corruption that this money buys is rotting fragile (failing) states.[56]

Such a relationship between state and nonstate actors provides numerous short- to mid-term benefits to both parties. As one example, the FARC (Colombia's major insurgent and drug-trafficking organization) gains access to Venezuelan territory and routes for exporting cocaine to Africa, Europe, and the United States. The FARC uses the same territory and routes to import weapons systems, communications equipment, training, and money. In this way, the Venezuelan government exerts indirect military pressure and related destabilization efforts on its most dangerous neighbor—Colombia. Additionally, the Venezuelan government enhances its international revolutionary credentials in the radical axis composed of leftist populists and Islamic fundamentalists. It is also able to profit from this illicit trade at a time when oil revenues are relatively low and the national budget is under significant stress. Given the enormous revenue stream that illicit Venezuelan-Colombian TCO trade represents, it is not likely that this alliance will go away soon.[57]

Clearly, the Venezuelan state and its criminal-insurgent-terrorist partners will continue to leverage their relationships to mutual benefit. But a cautionary note is required here. Over the long term, TCOs and criminal-insurgent networks have proven to be resilient and highly adaptable. This gives these kinds of actors an asymmetric advantage over partner state actors, which are inherently more bureaucratic, slow moving, and less adaptable than nonstate groups. At the same time, governments have also consistently underestimated the capabilities of more efficient nonhierarchical organizations. Those organizational advantages can generate a possible national security and sovereignty threat to the Venezuelan state in that national security and sovereignty are being impinged every day, and the illicit commercial motives of TCOs and other nonstate actors have been known to become a subtle and ominous political agenda. In short, the common putative objective of these hybrid horizontally organized nonstate groups is to control people, territory, and government to ensure their own freedom of movement and action within a given national territory (i.e., effective sovereignty).[58]

Increasing Economic Activity. At base, increasing economic activity is a continuation from the more fundamental alliance activity we call *Combating International Isolation.* Economic cooperation, as a result, has emerged as a defining feature of the alliance between Iran and the Chavez regime in Venezuela, and serves at least three clear purposes.

First, it allows Iran to circumvent financial sanctions imposed by the United States, the European Union (EU), and the United Nations (UN) through access to the Venezuelan financial system. As a consequence, Iran's partnership with Venezuela effectively provides an ancillary avenue from which it can access the international financial system, despite Western pressures. Second, this financial access facilitates the funding and support of radical populist and socialist parties and violent nonstate actors throughout the Hemisphere. Third, Iran has increased its economic investment in several areas (e.g., industry, mining, transportation, energy, and technical assistance). Many of Iran's contracts with various countries in Latin America have not yet come to fruition. The exception, however, is Venezuela, where substantial Iranian investments have been made. As a matter of fact, Iranian economic investment in Venezuela has expanded from virtually nothing in 2007 to a not insignificant $40 billion today.[59]

Even though much of the promised Iranian economic investment in the Hemisphere has not materialized, that country is in the process of creating an extensive regional network of diplomatic, economic, industrial, and commercial activities. Thus, probably the most dangerous threat to the United States from Venezuela results from its facilitation and encouragement of the penetration of the Western Hemisphere by Iran and its principal terrorist proxy, Hezbollah. Hezbollah has established a major regional presence throughout the Americas and is involved in a range of illicit activities, from drug trafficking, to money laundering, to training Venezuelan and other paramilitary forces.[60]

In this connection, coercive state and violent nonstate actors are serious impediments to growth, and major instruments for corrupting, distorting, and damaging stability in Latin America. The TCO-enforcer gang-insurgent-state nexus represents a triple threat to the authority and sovereignty of a host government as well as an enemy regime. First, murder, kidnapping, intimidation, corruption, and impunity undermine the ability of the state to perform its legitimizing security and public service functions. Second, by coercive imposition of power over bureaucrats and elected officials of the state, TCOs and their allies compromise the exercise of legitimate state authority and real democracy. Third, and closely related, by taking control of portions of a given national territory and performing at least some of the tasks of effective sovereign governance, the TCO phenomenon transforms itself *de facto* into states within the state, and criminal leaders govern as they wish. Thus, the hybrid TCO-state phenomenon contributes significantly to the erosion of democracy and to the evolutionary state failure process.[61]

Military-Paramilitary Presence in the Latin American Region. Military-Paramilitary presence builds on the previous two closely related elements of Hugo Chavez's "New Strategic Map for the Exportation of the Bolivarian Revolution" These actions facilitate serious regional instability through significant military equipment and arms purchases and training. They support extremists and various "liberation movements" in the Hemisphere and "generate economic production, influence, and angst."[62] In a world where public opinion is crucial, economic production, influence, and angst keep bourgeois enemies off balance and are great facilitators of long-term success (i.e., destabilization).

Military, paramilitary, and intelligence information is always among the murkiest areas of concern in global security politics. But even if complete and accurate information is not available, these issues cannot be prudently ignored. After all, governments do not invest long-term resources in pursuit of ephemeral or insubstantial aims. In that connection, Venezuela has submitted two reports to the UN Register of Conventional Arms (UNROCA), one in 1997 and the other in 2002. Both were nil. At the same time, even though Venezuela ratified the Organization of American States (OAS) Transparency Convention in 2005, it has never submitted a report. This was because of military secrecy laws; the 1999 Constitution gives the President of the Republic the right to classify and control disclosure of matters directly relating to the planning and execution of operations concerning national security. Additionally, in 2009, the National Assembly approved a law to maintain the confidentiality of military agreements between Venezuela and other states.[63] As a consequence, Venezuela has provided no information on weapons transfers from Russia either to UNROCA or the OAS. However, in 2012, Russia reported to the UNROCA that it had delivered 24 combat aircraft, 44 attack helicopters, and 2,272 missiles and missile launchers to Venezuela.[64]

Jane's Intelligence Weekly and *Jane's International Defense Review* report a good deal more. They state that Venezuela and Russia have signed agreements for arms and training over the period from 2004 to 2010 that amount to $11 billion. During that time, Venezuela received 24 Su-30MKV multirole fighters, 92 T-72 tanks, 57 transport and assault Mi-17/26/-35 helicopters, 25 CATIC K-8WB lead-in fighter trainers, four *Damen Stan Lander 5612* transport ships, and two *Stan Patrol 2602* coastal patrol craft. Other programs, coming to $4 billion, provide additional patrol vessels, armored personnel carriers (APCs), and BMP-3 infantry fighting vehicles. Additionally, Russia is supplying 24 BM-21 122 mm and 12 Smerch 300 mm multiple rocket launchers, 48 Sanyi 120 mm self-propelled mortars, 48 MSTA-S 152 mm self-propelled howitzers, and Buk-M2E mobile air defense systems. Lastly, more arms, long-range mobile radars, air defense systems, and electronic warfare centers are expected to be delivered in 2012.[65]

Accordingly, it is being reported that Russia is trying to regain the influential position it enjoyed in the 1970s and early-1980s in Latin America. At the same time, Russia is repaying Venezuela for its diplomatic recognition of the independence of Georgia's breakaway regions of Abkhazia and South Ossetia.[66] Whether or not these assertions can be proved is not as important as the fact that the reports of Venezuelan acquisition of these arms and weapons systems are destabilizing the military balance and causing a great deal of "angst" in Colombia, Guyana, and a few other countries in Latin America and the Caribbean regions.[67]

Russia, however, is not the only Venezuelan ally that maintains a military or paramilitary presence in Latin America. In addition to supporting Hezbollah, al-Qaeda, Hamas, and the Colombian FARC, the Iranian Quds force (the elite paramilitary unit of the Revolutionary Guards) has also placed operatives and trainers in embassies, charities, and Islamic religious and cultural institutions in the Hemisphere. The presumed intent is to enhance socioeconomic ties with the already well-established Shia Diaspora in the region, to collect intelligence and support extremists, and to help destabilize unfriendly regimes. Quds is also reportedly conducting training and support operations in Cuba, Bolivia, and Venezuela.[68] The organization that has reportedly received the most financial, arms, and training support from Quds is the Colombian

FARC and its political arm—the *Coordinadora Continental Bolivariana* (CCB). In addition to its political-psychological missions, the CCB maintains what some have called a "Foreign Legion."[69] Not surprisingly, the mission of the CCB Foreign Legion is to carry out paramilitary operations to support extremists and nascent and long-standing insurgent groups and to help destabilize bourgeois regimes. Consequently, the CCB is reported to be active in, at the least, Argentina, Bolivia, Brazil, Chile, Cuba, the Dominican Republic, Ecuador, Guatemala, Haiti, Honduras, Mexico, and Paraguay.[70]

Conclusions.

Some argue that all these agi-prop (agitation-propaganda) efforts aimed at the destabilization of bourgeois enemies and the organization of alliance activities are merely political theater. They are absolutely right. What they do not understand, however, is that 4th Generation Asymmetric Warfare is directed at influencing an unconventional center of gravity—that is, public opinion and leadership. As a consequence, it is important to understand that Hugo Chavez's Bolivarian Revolution is indeed political theater. It is intended to create political-economic-social disequilibrium, the weakening of an enemy state, and radical change over the long term. Accordingly, transition is grand strategic and epochal in scale. It ultimately witnesses change from the supposed misery of liberal democracy and capitalism to the promised love and harmony of "New Socialism."[71]

IMPLICATIONS AND RECOMMENDATIONS

In *The Sling and the Stone*, Colonel T. X. Hammes, USMC (Ret.), argues that "Just as the world has evolved from an industrial society to an information-based society, so has warfare."[72] 4GW does not attempt to win wars by defeating an enemy's military forces. Both the epic, decisive Napoleonic battle (2nd Generation War), and the wide-ranging, high-tech, high-speed maneuver campaign (3rd Generation War—"Shock and Awe") are irrelevant. 4GW is an evolved form of insurgency rooted in the fundamental precept that superior political will, when properly employed, can defeat greater military and economic power. It uses all available networks—political, economic, social, informational, and military—to convince the enemy decisionmakers that their goals are either unachievable or too costly to justify the perceived benefits. Using its networks, 4GW directly attacks the minds of enemy populations, policymakers, and decisionmakers to destroy their political will.[73]

These are the principal characteristics of what President Hugo Chavez of Venezuela has called "4th Generation War," "Guerra de todo el pueblo ("War of all the People," "Peoples' War," or "War Among Peoples"). He asserts that this type of conflict has virtually unlimited possibilities for a "Super Insurgency" intended to bring about fundamental political-economic-social change in the Western Hemisphere.[74] The urgency and importance of the 4GW threat have generated four related themes. First, several countries in Latin America and the Caribbean are paradigms of the failing state and have enormous implications for the stability, development, democracy, prosperity, and peace of the entire Western Hemisphere. Second, the transnational drug and arms trafficking, paramilitary, insurgent, and gang organizations in Mexico, Central and South America, and the Caribbean Basin are perpetrating a level of corruption, criminality, human horror, and internal instability that, if left unchecked at the strategic level, can ultimately threaten the collapse of various states and undermine the security and sovereignty of neighbors. Third, poverty, social exclusion, environmental degradation, and political-economic-social expectations—and the conflicts generated by these indirect and implicit threats to stability and human well-being—lead to further degeneration of citizen security. Fourth, these threats also constitute a serious challenge of U.S. national security, well-being, and position in the global community.

The primary implication of the complex and ambiguous situations described above is straightforward. The contemporary, chaotic global strategic environment reflects a general lack of legitimate governance and civil-military cooperation in many parts of the world. Instability thrives under those conditions. Instability, violence, terrorism, and criminal anarchy are the general consequences of unreformed political, social, economic, and security institutions and concomitant misguided or poor governance. Ultimately, this instability, and the human, nonstate, and state destabilizers who exploit it, lead to a final downward spiral into failing and failed-state status. Again, it must be remembered that, as important as instability might be, it is only a symptom—not the threat itself. Again, the ultimate threat is the issue nobody wants to deal with—state failure.

The novelist John le Carré succinctly defines a failing or failed state in stark terms:

> I would suggest to you that, these days, very roughly, the qualifications for being a *civilized state* amount to — electoral suffrage . . . protection of life and property . . . justice, health and education for all . . . the maintenance of a sound administrative structure — and roads, transport, drains, etcetera — and — what else is there? — ah yes, the equitable collection of taxes. If a state fails to deliver on at least a quorum of the above — then one *has* to say that the contract between state and citizen begins to look pretty *shaky* — and if it fails on *all* of the above, then it's a *failed state* . . . an unstate . . . an ex-state."[75]

The logic of the state failure situation demonstrates that the conscious choices that the international community and individual nation-states make about how to deal with this type of unconventional threat will define the processes of national, regional, and global security and well-being for now and into the future. This cautionary tale reminds us that protracted asymmetric war (4GW) is the only kind of conflict that a modern power has ever lost. It is surprising and dismaying that the world's only superpower does not have a unified long-term strategy and a multidimensional interagency organizational architecture to deal with Chavez's 21st-Century Socialism and its associated asymmetric war.[76] It would appear that this epochal transitional threat is being dismissed as too difficult, too ambiguous, and too far into the future to deal with. Nevertheless, prudence dictates that it is time to take the empirical evidence seriously and make substantive political-economic, social, informational, and military changes to deal effectively with the threat that one dare not speak its name.[77]

The primary challenge, then, is to come to terms with the pressing need to shift from a singular operational-tactical military-police approach to a multidimensional and multinational paradigm. That, in turn, requires a strategic-level conceptual framework and a supporting organizational structure to promulgate unified civil-military planning and the implementation of transnational responses to transnational threats. These efforts must be organized as a network rather than in the traditional vertical, top-down bureaucracies of most governments. Accomplishing such efforts will also require fundamental changes in how government leaders and personnel at all levels are employed, trained, developed, and promoted. Additionally, and most importantly, this interagency and multilateral process must exert its collective influence for the entire duration of a conflict — from the initial planning to the final achievement (or compulsion) of a sustainable peace. Remember, it is the last man standing — regardless of how badly beaten he might be — who is the winner in this type of conflict.

Recommendations.

Long lists of recommendations and measures of effectiveness will be irrelevant if the strategic-level conceptual and architectural foundational requirements are not implemented first. One of Carl von Clausewitz's translators, Michael Howard, warned us years ago, "If [the political-psychological struggle] is not conducted with skill and based on realistic analysis . . . no amount of operational expertise, logistical backup, or technology could possibly help."[78] Nevertheless, there are a few high-level recommendations the U.S. Army could propose, and some more intermediate-level recommendations it could implement.

- High-Level Recommendations:
  - The Army could recommend a permanent interagency end-state planning capability. This capability should include transnational coordination and cooperation.
  - The Army could recommend an updated executive-legislative understanding of the purpose of U.S. security and guidelines for amendments to the Foreign Assistance Act of 1961, in accordance with the new requirements of the nonkinetic tools of statecraft.
  - The Army could help plan and implement indirect and direct actions against belligerent and politicized nonstate actors using Foreign Area Officer (FAO) diagnosticians with appropriate political-cultural literacy and language skills.
  - At the least, the Army could develop a design for using conventional armed forces in nontraditional roles mandated by the new sociology of deliberate conflict outlined above in Chavez's Asymmetric Warfare Model, and the Paramilitary Operational Model for Compelling Radical Change. The Army could also develop a design for conflict based on the Chavez/Venezuelan model that is also being inadvertently used by belligerent and politicized non-state actors.[79] Such a redefinition of mission, organization, and training would be useful in informing military reform debates in Latin America and elsewhere that still cling to the Westphalian model of sovereignty and warfare.[80]

- Intermediate-Level Recommendations for Leader Development and Professional Military Education:
  - The study of the fundamental nature of conflict has always been the philosophical cornerstone for comprehending the essence of traditional conflict. It is no less relevant to unconventional war.
  - Leaders at all levels must understand the strategic and political implications of tactical and operational-level actions. They must also understand the ways that military force can be employed to achieve political and psychological ends and understand and accept the ways that political considerations affect the use of force.
  - Leaders must acquire the ability to interact collegially and effectively with U.S. civilian agencies, representatives of international organizations, nongovernmental organizations (NGOs), local and global news media, and civilian populations.
  - Leaders must understand that information and intelligence, and psychological and public diplomacy activities, are force multipliers. Professional military education and leader development must foster the concept that commanders at all levels have to take responsibility for collecting and managing human intelligence and conducting public diplomacy efforts for their own use. Also, they must understand the penalties that are paid when these instrument of power are ignored.

— Lastly, education and training for contemporary unconventional conflict must prepare military personnel to be effective war-fighters. Additionally, because of the highly charged political-psychological environment in which military personnel must now work, combatants must also display political-cultural sensitivity, considerable restraint, and strong discipline. Again, combatants must understand the price they will pay if a population should become alienated.[81]

• Lastly, the above recommendations can, *inter alia*, provide the bases for policy direction for:
  — Security cooperation and building partnership capability.
  — Strategic communications in terms of exchanging key messages or themes on a host of mutually important topics.
  — Institutional and professional development between the U.S. Army and its international partners.
  — Enhancing personnel exchange programs and political-cultural-language skills.
  — Criminal-Transnational Criminal Organizations (C-TCO) training to improve professional competence of partner armies, while at the same time following the rule of law and the human rights of their citizens.[82]

Difficult as these recommendations may be to implement, they are far less demanding and costly in political, military, and monetary terms than the conventional approach. The author of *The Sling and the Stone* reminds us that allowing the age-old "business as usual" and "crisis management" approaches to work at cross-purposes with the reality of contemporary unconventional asymmetric conflict is a sure formula for failure in generating global stability and security.[83] However, a final cautionary note is in order. The U.S. Army and other U.S. military forces must educate, organize, equip, and train to deal with an unpredictable enemy. Thus, the study of chaos, ambiguity, complexity, and flexibility must be essential elements in the education and development of strategic leaders. The most likely situation to arise in unconventional asymmetric conflict is that it might not be foreseen or planned for.[84]

ENDNOTES

1. President Chavez used this language in a charge to the National Armed Forces (FAN) to develop a doctrine for 4th Generation Asymmetric War. It was made before an audience gathered in the Military Academy Auditorium for the "1st Military Forum on Fourth Generation and Asymmetric War," in Caracas, Venezuela, and was reported in *El Universal,* April 8, 2005.

2. In 2007, we emphasized Venezuelan President Hugo Chavez's adaption of asymmetric war and summarized its consequences by taking a page from a Harry Potter adventure. See Max G. Manwaring, *Latin America's New Security Reality: Irregular Asymmetric Conflict and Hugo Chavez*, Carlisle, PA: Strategic Studies Institute, U.S. Army War College, 2007, pp. 37-38. We characterized Chavez as a metaphorical "Master" of asymmetric war. In Harry Potter's first adventure, he was cautioned by his friends to never speak the name of the cunning and evil main antagonist in the entire series of adventures. See J. K. Rowling, *Harry Potter and the Sorcerer's Stone*, New York: Arthur A. Levine Books, 1997, pp. 11, 54-57.

3. Erik Becker Becker, "Chavez: una incision en la historia de Venezuela" ("Chavez: a sharp stimulation in the history of Venezuela"), *Dialogo Politico*, December 2003, pp. 155-174; Heinz Dieterick, "Nace la Doctrina Militar de la Revolucion Venezuelana" ("A Military Doctrine Emerges for the Venezuelan Revolution"), December 17, 2004, available from *www.aporrea.org/actualidad/ a11176.html*; "Special Report: Hugo Chavez's Venezuela," *The Economist*, May 14-20, 2005, p. 25; Steve Ellner, "Revolutionary and Non-Revolutionary Paths of Radical Populism: Directions of the Chavez Movement in Venezuela," *Science and Society*, April 2005, pp. 160-190; Andres Benavente Urbina and Julio Alberto Cirino, "El populismo Chavista en Venezuela" ("Chavista populism in Venezuela"), in *La democracia defraudada*, Buenos Aires, Argentina: Grito Sagrado, 2005, pp. 115-139; Julio Alblert Cirino, "La Revolucion Mundial Pasa Por Hugo Chavez" ("World Revolution Will Go Through Hugo Chavez"), Part 1, in *Panorama*, April 20, 2005 and Part 2, April 27, 2005; Manuel Cabieses, "Donde va Chavez? Una entrevista al president venezolano" ("Where is Chavez going? An interview with the Venezuelan president"), October 19, 2005, available from *www.alterinfos.org/article.php3?id_article=66*; Adolfo R. Tayihardat, "La exportacion de la revolucion Bolivariana" ("The exportation of the Bolivarian revolution"), October 3, 2005, available from *www.analitica.com/va/internacionalels/ opinikon/1693165.asp*; Alvaro Vargas Llosa, "The Return of Latin America's Left," *The New York Times*, March 22, 2005; and "The Chavez Machine Rolls On," *The Economist*, December 2, 2006, pp. 41-42.

4. William Neuman, "Chavez Says His Cancer Shows Signs of Return," *The New York Times*, February 22, 2012, p. A4.

5. See Endnote 2, above. Also see Leopoldo E. Colmenares, "Implicancias de los Movimentos Populistas" ("Implication of Populist Movements"), unpublished manuscript, presented at the Centro de Estudios Hemisfericos de Defense, Washington, DC, July, 10-13, 2007.

6. Lenin said that a "new society" will only be created by gradual and systematic application of agitation and propaganda. See V. I. Lenin, "The Tasks of the Russian Social Democrats," in Robert C. Tucker, ed., *The Lenin Anthology*, New York: W. W. Norton & Company, 1975, p. 4. Also see Lenin, "Speech in Closing the Congress, April 2, 1922, p. 533.

7. *The Economist*, "The 2008 and 2010 Latinobarometro Polls," November 15, 2008, pp. 46-47, and December 4, 2010, p. 51.

8. Joshua Kucera, "What is Hugo Chavez Up To?" *Wilson Quarterly*, Spring 2011, pp. 22-30.

9. Cirino, "populismo Chavista," 2005; and "Chavez mete mas presion," 2005.

10. *Ibid.* Also see *The Economist*, "Special Report: Hugo Chavez's Venezuela," May 14-20, 2005, pp. 23-24; *The Economist*, "The Chavez Machine Rolls On," December 2, 2006, pp. 41-42; *The Economist*, "Chavez Victorious," December 9, 2006; and Ellner, "Revolutions," 2005.

11. Jean Jacques Rousseau, *The Social Contract* [1762], G. D. H. Cole, trans., Chicago, IL: Encyclopedia Britannica, Inc., 1952. Also see Jacques Maritain, *Man and the State*, Chicago, IL: University of Chicago Press, 1951, pp. 13-27, 192 .

12. *Ibid.*

13. Steven Metz and Douglas V. Johnson II, *Asymmetry and U.S. Military Strategy: Definition, Background, and Strategic Concepts*, Carlisle, PA: Strategic Studies Institute, U.S. Army War College, 2001, pp. 5-6.

14. Steven Metz, "Relearning Counterinsurgency," a panel discussion at the American Enterprise Institute, January 10, 2005. Also see Paul E. Smith, *On Political War*, Washington, DC: National Defense University Press, 1989.

15. "War of All the People" is another translation of Hugo Chavez's words in this context. Thus, he interchangeably uses 4th Generation War, Super Insurgency, People's War, Asymmetric War, and War of All the People.

16. *Jane's Military and Security Assessments*, "Venezuela at a Glance," December 12, 2011. Also see *International Crisis Group*, "Violence and Politics in Venezuela — Militias," Latin American Report No. 38, August 17, 2011, pp. 26-27.

17. Reported in *El Universal*, January 5, 2005; *El Universal*, March 8, 2005; *Europa Press*, April 3, 2005, *La Voz*, April 3, 2005; *El Universal*, April 8, 2005; Taylherdat; and *The Economist*, "The Americas: A Caribbean Tripoli? Venezuela's Militias," April 9, 2011, p. 44. Also see General Gustavo Reyes Rangel Briceno's speech when he accepted the post of Ministro del Poder Popular para la Defensa (the paramilitary forces of Venezuela), July 18, 2007.

18. Michael Shifter, "In Search of Hugo Chavez," *Foreign Affairs*, May/June 2006, p. 46; *The Economist*, "Chavez Victorious," December 9, 2006; and Michael Shifter, "Hugo Chavez: A Test for U.S. Policy," Washington, DC: *Interamerican Dialogue*, March 2007; and *The Washington Post*, "Venezuela Lets Councils Bloom," May 16, 2007.

19. Stephen Johnson, "South America's Mad-TV: Hugo Chavez Makes Broadcasting a Battleground," *The Heritage Foundation Policy Research & Analysis,* August 10, 2005, *Foreign Broadcast Information Service (FBIS),* "New Regional Voice," April 22, 2005; *FBIS* "Expanded Telesur News Coverage Furthers Anti-US Line," December 22, 2005; *FBIS*, "Perspective Audience," August 5, 2006; and *FBIS,* "Telesur's Deal with Al-Jazirah," February 27, 2006. Also see "Iran launches Spanish TV channel," *The Guardian*, January 31, 2012, available from *www.guardian.co.uk/world/2012/jan/31/iran-launches-spanish-tv-channel/print*.

20. Thomas A. Marks, "Ideology and Insurgency," *Small Wars & Insurgencies*, Spring 2004, pp. 107-109.

21. Carl von Clausewitz, *On War*, Michael Howard and Peter Paret, trans. and eds., New Brunswick, NJ: Princeton University Press, [1832] 1976, p. 596.

22. *Ibid.* Also see *The Economist*, "Special Report: Hugo Chavez's Venezuela," May 14-20, 2005, pp. 23-24.

23. Lenin, "Tasks of Social Democrats," p. 4.

24. *Ibid.*, pp. 4-5.

25. *Ibid.*, pp. 6-7.

26. *Ibid.* Also see Lenin, "The State and Revolution," p. 324.

27. Lenin, "On Revolutionary Violence and Terror," p. 425.

28. Colonel T. X. Hammes, USMC (Ret.), *The Sling and the Stone*, St. Paul, MN: Zenith Press, 2006.

29. Lenin, "Socialism and War," p. 188.

30. Smith, *Utility of Force*, 2007.

31. Qiao Liang and Wang Xiangsui, *Unrestricted Warfare*, Beijing, China: PLA Arts and Literature Publishing House, 1999, pp. 143, 157.

32. *Ibid.*

33. *Ibid.*, p. 154.

34. *Ibid.*, pp. 41, 123. Also see Roger Trinquier, *Modern Warfare: A French View of Counterinsurency*, Ft. Leavenworth, KS: Combined Arms Research Library, 1964, p. 35.

35. See Endnote 2.

36. Lenin, "Capitalist Discords and Concessions Policy," pp. 628-634.

37. *Sendero Luminoso's* former leader, Abimael Guzman, made that particular statement in "El Discurso del Dr. Guzman" ("Dr. Guzman's Speech"), Rogger Mercade U., ed., *Los partidos politics en el Peru* (*Political parties in Peru*), Lima, Peru: Edicones Latino-americanos, 1985, pp. 85-90.

38. Chavez interview with Manuel Cabieses, *Punta Final*, October 19, 2005. Also see Abraham Guillen, *Philosphy of the Urban Guerrilla: The Revolutionary Writings of Abraham Guillen*, Donald C. Hodges, ed. and trans., New York: William Morrow, 1973, pp. 231, 249, 253, 279, 283.

39. Lenin, "Report on War and Peace," pp. 545-546, 549.

40. Qiao and Wang, 1999, p. 109.

41. The idea of Wizard's Chess is taken from J. K. Rowling, *Harry Potter and the Sorcerer's Stone*, 1997, pp. 282-284. Also see Max G. Manwaring, "The New Master of Wizard's Chess: The Real Hugo Chavez and Asymmetric Warfare," *Military Review*, September-October, 2005, pp. 40-49.

42. Robert J. Bunker, "Grand Strategic Overview: Epochal Change and New Realities for the United States," *Small Wars & Insurgencies*, December 2011, pp. 728-733.

43. Guillen, "Philosophy," pp. 233, 279.

44. President Chavez has adopted Jorge Verstrynge's book, *Peripheral Warfare and Revolutionary Islam: Origins, Rules, and Ethics of Asymmetrical Warfare.* He liked the book so much that he had a special edition printed and distributed to the Venezuelan officer corps with express orders to read it, learn from it, and develop new asymmetric war doctrine. Verstrynge argues that the destruction of the United States will come about when its vast conventional military might cannot be used to combat its asymmetric enemies effectively. See Verstrynge, *Peripheral Warfare and Revolutionary Islam: Origins, Rules, and Ethics of Asymmetrical Warfare*, Madrid, Spain: El Viejo Topo, May 2005.

45. See General Briceno's speech, dated July 18, 2007. Also see J. Boyer Bell, *Dragonwars*, New Brunswick, NJ: Transaction Publishers, 1999, pp. 417-418.

46. Briceno speech, July 18, 2007.

47. *Ibid.*

48. Daniel C. Esty, Jack Goldstone, Ted Robert Gurr, Barbara Harff, and Pamela T. Surko, "The State Failure Project: Early Warning Research for U.S. Foreign Policy Planning," John L. Davies and Ted Robert Gurr, eds., *Preventive Measures: Building Risk Assessment and Crisis Early Warning Systems*, New York: Rowman & Littlefield Publishers, 1998.

49. Steven D. Krasner and Carlos Pascal, "Addressing State Failure," *Foreign Affairs*, July/August 2005, pp. 153-155. Also see Chester A Crocker, "Engaging Failed States," *Foreign Affairs*, September/October 2003, pp. 32-44; and Steven D. Krasner, "An Orienting Principle for Foreign Policy," *Policy Review*, No. 163, Hoover Institution, Stanford University, October 2010.

50. Krasner and Pascual, "Addressing State Failure," 2005.

51. Charles W. Kegley, Jr., and Eugene R. Wittkopf, *World Politics: Trends and Transformation*, 6th Ed., New York: St. Martin's Press, 1997, pp. 443-447.

52. Taylhardat, "La Exportacion," 2005.

53. Ilan Berman, testimony before the U.S. Senate Committee on Foreign Relations Subcommittee on Western Hemisphere, Peace Corps, and Global Narcotics Affairs, February 16, 2012; and Norman A. Bailey, testimony before the Committee on Foreign Affairs, House of Representatives, February 2, 2012. Also see Douglas Farah, "Terrorist-Criminal Pipelines and Criminalized States: Emerging Alliances, *PRISM* 2, No. 3, June 2011; and "Las FARC mantienan contactos con grupos armadas Bolivarianos de Venezuela desde 2002" ("The Revolutionary Armed Forces of Colombia (FARC) have maintained contacts with Bolivarian armed groups in Venezuela since 2002"), *El Tiempo*, February 9, 2010.

54. Dieterich.

55. Farah, "Pipelines," 2011.

56. David C. Jordan, *Drug Politics: Dirty Money and Democracies*, Norman, OK: University of Oklahoma Press, 1999.

57. Farah, "Pipelines," 2011.

58. John P. Sullivan and Robert J. Bunker, "Drug Cartels, Street Gangs, and Warlords," *Nonstate Threats and Future Wars*, Robert J. Bunker, ed., London, UK: Frank Cass, 2003, pp. 40-53; John P. Sullivan, "Terrorism, Crime, and Private Armies," *Low Intensity Conflict & Law Enforcement*, Winter 2002, pp. 239-253; and

Max G. Manwaring, *Street Gangs: The New Urban Insurgency,* Carlisle, PA: Strategic Studies Institute, U.S. Army War College, 2005.

59. Bailey and Berman, "Testimonies," 2012.

60. *Ibid.*

61. John P. Sullivan, "Maras Morphing: Revisiting Third Generation Gangs," *Global Crime*, August-November, 2006, pp. 488-490.

62. Joshua Kucera, "What is Hugo Chavez Up To?" *The Wilson Quarterly*, Spring 2011.

63. Reported in *El Universal*, September 23, 2009.

64. Constitution of the Bolivarian Republic of Venezuela, December 30, 1999, Article 325. Also see Mark Bromley and Carina Solmirano, *Transparency in Military Spending and Arms Acquisitions in Latin America and the Caribbean*, Stockholm, Sweden: Stockholm International Peace Research Institute (SIPRI), January 2012, pp. 31-32.

65. *Jane's Intelligence Weekly*, The Americas, posted August 12, 2011; and *Jane's International Defense Review*, International Defense Digest, posted October 21, 2011.

66. *Ibid.*

67. *Ibid.* Also, Author Interviews conducted in Latin America in July and August 2009.

68. Bailey and Berman "Testimonies," 2012; Farah, "Pipelines," 2011; Office of the Secretary of Defense, unclassified report on the Military Power of Iran, April 2010; and "Iran and Latin America: Brothers in Arms?" *The Economist*, January 14, 2012, p. 36.

69. Doug Farah, *Traditional Organized Crime, Criminalized States, and Terrorism in Latin America*, Carlisle, PA: Strategic Studies Institute, U.S. Army War College, 2012, p. 41.

70. Author Interviews, July and August 2009, in Bogota, Colombia; Lima, Peru; and Santiago, Chile.

71. Briceno speech, July 18, 2007.

72. Hammes, *The Sling and the Stone*, 2006, p. i.

73. *Ibid.*, pp. 1, 210, 246-257.

74. Chavez used this language in a charge to the National Armed Forces to develop a doctrine for 4GW. See Endnote 2.

75. John le Carré, *The Constant Gardner*, New York: Scribner, 2001, p. 137.

76. Hammes, *The Sling and the Stone*, 2006; and "Fourth Generation Warfare," *Armed Forces Journal*, November 2004, pp. 40-44.

77. See Endnote 2.

78. Michael Howard, *The Causes of War*, 2nd Ed., Cambridge, MA: Harvard University Press, 1983, p. 109.

79. Author Interviews with Carter, Galvin, Wilhelm, and General James T. Hill, USAR (Ret.), in Carlisle, PA, Strategic Studies Institute, U.S. Army War College, October 2003. Also see Bunker, "Grand Strategic Overview," December, 2011.

80. *Ibid.*

81. *Ibid.*

82. *Ibid.*

83. Hammes, *The Sling and the Stone*, pp. i, 14-15.

84. General Frank Kiston (UK, Ret.), *Warfare as a Whole*, London, UK: Faber and Faber, 1987, p. 61.